P9-DDT-054

Spain

Anita Croy

José Manuel Reyes and Raquel Medina

NATIONAL GEOGRAPHIC
WASHINGTON, D.C.

Cuyahoga Falls Library
Cuyahoga Falls, Ohio

Contents

Foreword

For many people, Spain is known as the land of flamenco dancing, beautiful beaches, and bullfighting. With over 60 million tourists each year, this large European nation is the second most visited country in the world. However, much of Spain remains largely unknown to foreigners.

Spain is located on the Iberian Peninsula, which lies in the southwestern part of Europe and is only eight miles (13 km) from northern Africa. It is surrounded by the Mediterranean Sea and the Atlantic Ocean. Spain's location between two continents has been an important factor in its history and culture.

In early times different Mediterranean peoples, such as Phoenicians, Greeks, and Romans, settled the Iberian Peninsula and introduced new beliefs, ideas, and customs throughout the course of history. During the Middle Ages, the land was divided into different Christian and Muslim kingdoms, which alternated between periods of peaceful coexistence and war until 1492. That year became a turning point in Spain's history, for it marked the conquest of the last Muslim kingdom, the end of the country's Jewish community, and the beginning of the colonization of the Americas.

The most enduring contribution of Spain to the world is the Spanish language, taken to the Americas with the expansion of the Empire in the 16th century. Nowadays about 400 million people speak Spanish in 22 countries, including 35 million who speak it at home in the United States. The Spanish language is a significant influence around the world.

During the past 50 years, Spain has undergone a huge economic, social, and cultural transformation. After a tragic civil war and a 40-year dictatorship, Spain has now become a lively democracy that embraces its

many regional identities, cultural differences, and a large population of immigrants from around the world. The Spanish people are trying to find a balance between their traditional way of life, where family, friends, and hometown are very important, and the new values they encounter as they meet people from other countries. This book is a great introduction to the geography and nature, history and government, and people and culture of this most passionate and intriguing country.

▲ The outside of Casa Batllo in Barcelona was remodeled by the famous architect Antoni Gaudí in 1907. Much of the front of the building is covered in a mosaic of broken colored tiles.

José Manuel Reyes
Hanover College,
United States of America

A Land Between Seas

SPAIN IS THE LARGEST OF THREE COUNTRIES in the Iberian Peninsula. The peninsula forms the westernmost region of Europe and also contains Portugal on the western coast and tiny Andorra in the Pyrenees Mountains. The soaring peaks of the Pyrenees along Spain's border with France are the only link with mainland Europe. The rest of the peninsula is surrounded by sea. Since the Pyrenees are such a formidable barrier in the north, Spain shares much of its early history with Africa, which is located across the Strait of Gibraltar to the south.

Centuries ago, the area of present-day Spain was broken into small kingdoms kept separate by mountain ranges. Back then the oceans linked Spain with the rest of Europe, and it was the oceans that led Spanish explorers to the vast riches of the Americas.

◀ **The Montserrat Mountains near Barcelona are a favorite hiking spot.**

WHAT'S THE WEATHER LIKE?

Spain has three main climate areas: the coasts, the mountains, and the Meseta—a plateau in central Spain. Nevertheless there are dramatic differences in weather across the country. Spain is Europe's sunniest country, but in Galicia in the northwest, it rains frequently all year. In the far south the climate is dry, with hot summers and only a little rain falling in winter. The capital, Madrid, has an extreme climate. Summer temperatures above 105° F (40° C) are common, while in winter they tumble below freezing.

The map opposite shows Spain's physical features. Labels on this map and on similar maps throughout this book identify most of the places pictured in each chapter.

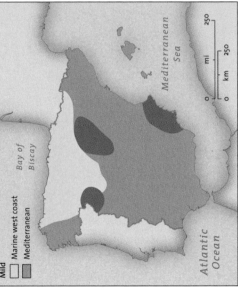

MAP KEY
Dry
Semiarid
Mild
Marine west coast
Mediterranean

Bay of Biscay

Mediterranean Sea

Atlantic Ocean

mi   250
km   250

Fast Facts

Official Name: Kingdom of Spain

Type of Government: Parliamentary monarchy

Capital: Madrid

Population: 46,157,822

Official Language: Castilian Spanish

Monetary Unit: Euro

Area: 194,896 sq miles (504,782 sq km)

Borders: France, Andorra, Gibraltar (UK), Morocco, Portugal

Highest Point: Mulhacén, 11,411 feet (3,480 meters; mainland); Pico de Teide, 12,195 feet (3,718 meters; Tenerife)

Lowest Point: Atlantic Ocean, 0 feet (0 meters)

Major Mountain Ranges: Pyrenees, Sierra Nevada, Cantabrian Mountains

Major Rivers: Guadalquivir, Duero, Tajo, Guadiana, and Ebro

Average Temperature & Rainfall

Average High/Low Temperatures; Yearly Rainfall

Madrid (central): 76° F (24° C) / 41° F (5° C); 26 in (66 cm)

Almería (south): 78° F (26° C) / 54° F (12° C); 0.25 in (0.7 cm)

Soria (north): 68° F (20° C) / 36° F (2° C); 43 in (107 cm)

Gran Canaria (Canary Islands): 75° F (24° C) / 63° F (17° C); 1 in (2.5 cm)

Physical Map

MAP KEY

⊛ National capital

• Selected city

+ Elevation

COASTAL INLET, page 11

PEOPLE SHELTER FROM RAIN, page 10

FLOCK OF SHEEP, page 11

RIVER PASSES HILLTOP TOWN, page 15

FARMHOUSE BELOW JAGGED MOUNTAINS, pages 2, 6–7

WINDMILLS, page 12

ACTOR IN WESTERN MOVIE SET, page 15

ROCKY HEADLAND, page 13

miles 150

km 150

FRANCE

ANDORRA

ALGERIA

MOROCCO

PORTUGAL

S P A I N

GALICIA

LA MANCHA

Madrid

A Coruña
Santiago de Compostela
Vigo
Gijón
Santander
Bilbao
Valladolid
Zaragoza
Barcelona
Toledo
Valencia
Alicante
Murcia
Córdoba
Almería
Tabernas
Málaga
Seville
Tarifa
Ceuta
Melilla
Palma de Mallorca

Cordillera Cantábrica (Cantabrian Mountains)

Pyrenees

Aneto 11,168 ft 3,404 m

Mallos de Riglos

Sierra Nevada
Mulhacén 11,413 ft 3,479 m

GIBRALTAR (U.K.)

Peñón de Vélez de la Gomera
Peñón de Alhucemas
Islas Chafarinas
Isla de Alborán

Bay of Biscay

Atlantic Ocean

Mediterranean Sea

Balearic Islands
Menorca
Mallorca
Ibiza

Cape Trafalgar

Strait of Gibraltar

Rivers: Sil, Duero, Douro (Tagus), Tejo (Tagus), Esla, Tagus (Tajo), Guadiana, Guadalquivir, Ebro, Jalón, Júcar, Segura, Turia, Llobregat

VOLCANIC CRATER, page 14

Pico de Teide (Highest point in Spain) 12,195 ft 3,718 m

BEACH WITH BLACK SAND, page 12

La Palma
Gomera
Hierro
Tenerife
Gran Canaria
Las Palmas
Fuerteventura
Lanzarote

Canary Islands

mi 50

km 50

Europe
Africa
SPAIN
Atlantic Ocean

▲ A hiker stands above a mountain lake fed by the melting snow of the Spanish Pyrenees.

▼ The rainy city of Santiago on the edge of the Cantabrian Mountains is the umbrella-making center of Spain.

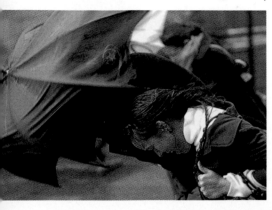

High Plains and Peaks

Spain is one of the most mountainous countries in Europe. Much of the rest of the country is covered by plateaus. The only lowlands are a few narrow coastal plains and river valleys.

There are three main mountain ranges in Spain. The largest range is the Pyrenees, which stretches across the neck of land between the Mediterranean Sea and the Atlantic Ocean that joins Spain to France. The Sierra Nevada is the main southern range. The highest point on mainland Spain (Mulhacén) is located there. (The country's highest peak of all is in the Canaries—a group of islands in the Atlantic.) The third range is the Cantabrian Mountains near the northern coast. These mountains catch much of the rain coming in from the ocean.

Inland Plateau

Much of inland Spain is a plateau called the Meseta. This region covers around 40 percent of the country. The land lies between 1,300 and 3,300 feet (400 and 1,000 m) above sea level, and there are few hills and mountains to break up the landscape.

▲ The northern Meseta is mostly used as a pasture for sheep.

ANCIENT LANDSCAPE

The province of Galicia, in the far northwest corner of Spain, has a climate more like that of northern Europe than the rest of the country. The weather is often wet, and nothing like the hot dry summers of the Spanish plains to the south.

The distinctive landscape of the Galician coast was formed during the last ice age, when the region was covered in glaciers. The glaciers carved out wide valleys, which have now been flooded by rising sea levels. These inlets are known as *rías* (above) and are the Spanish version of the sea lochs of Scotland and the fiords of Norway.

A STAIN ON THE LAND

Two of the most famous and popular characters in Spanish literature are Don Quixote and his sidekick, Sancho Panza. They are characters in a 1605 novel by Miguel de Cervantes, who put a wild and desolate region of Spain on the map. La Mancha, which means "the stain," is the name used for a dry part of the Meseta between Madrid and Valencia. The windmills in La Mancha were used to power the mills that grind wheat grown in the region into flour.

▲ In Cervantes's novel, Don Quixote is a noble but dim-witted knight. He attacks windmills thinking they are giants.

▼ Sunbathers relax on an unusual beach in the Canary Islands: The volcanic sand is black!

The mountains circling the Meseta block many of the rain clouds from reaching the area. The northern plateau receives some rain, but the south is so dry it is semidesert in places. Few people live in the Meseta and there are only sheep for company. It is difficult to grow crops there, but livestock farming is common. The region is nicknamed the "belly" of Spain because it produces so many meat products.

Along the Coast

For most tourists who visit Spain, the only part of the country they see is the coast. Thanks to the miles of beautiful sandy beaches and warm sea that stretch all the way down the Mediterranean and Atlantic shores, tourism is one of Spain's biggest industries. However, from the rugged inlets of Galicia in the north to the towering Rock of Gibraltar in the south, the long coastlines have a lot more to offer.

The coastal strip contains the most fertile land in Spain. Citrus fruits and grapes are two of the major crops grown there. Small rivers that flow into the Mediterranean, such as the Segura, Turia, and Llobregat, provide the irrigation water for these crops as well as rice and other grains. The lush Mediterranean coast is known as the "rice bin" of Spain.

Sun-Soaked Islands

Formed from ancient volcanoes, the Canary Islands are much closer to the North African coast than they are to Spain. One island, Fuerteventura, is just 60 miles (97 km) off the northwest coast of Africa and about 820 miles (1,320 km) from Spain. There are seven major islands, of which Tenerife is the largest.

▼ The Rock of Gibraltar is a huge piece of limestone that rises above the sea near the southern tip of Spain. The rock is a territory of the United Kingdom and has a crowded city and naval base.

The second largest island, Fuerteventura, is flat and dry while the third biggest, Gran Canaria, has the biggest city of all the islands, Las Palmas. The Canary Islands are subtropical and enjoy warm weather all year round, making them a favorite tourist destination.

Another island group—the Balearic Islands—is located to the east of the Spanish mainland in the Mediterranean Sea. About 150 miles (240 km) out are the two largest islands, Mallorca (Majorca) and Menorca. Ibiza, the third-largest member of the group, is considerably closer—only 50 miles (80 km) from Spain. Tourists flock to the Balearics for beach vacations or to relax in the cool mountains.

River Basins

Despite Spain's huge size there are only a few large rivers. As a result, water is a very precious commodity,

ROCKY ISLANDS

The Canary Islands lie off the coast of Morocco but have belonged to Spain since 1479. The archipelago has seven islands and many tiny islets. It is named for the songbirds that originally came from the islands and are now kept as pets across the world. The islands contain the highest peak in Spain, the Pico de Teide on the largest of the islands, Tenerife. The Canaries are a popular vacation destination, but geologists are interested in them for another reason. Some think that the island of La Palma might one day break apart and cause a huge tsunami that could drown the eastern seaboard of the United States.

▲ A catastrophic eruption of this volcano on La Palma might cause a devastating tsunami one day.

THE WILD WEST—IN SPAIN!

It might come as a surprise to learn that many of the most popular Western movies were not filmed in America but in southern Spain! The desert town of Tabernas in the region of Andalusia has provided the set for many classic movies, such as *A Fistful of Dollars* in 1964. The dry and barren landscape is a good stand-in for the deserts of the Southwest. The Spanish location was chosen because it was much less expensive than those in the United States. One film set is now a theme park where tourists tour the Wild West saloons and watch mock gunfights and bank robberies.

▲ An actor plays the part of a cowboy arriving in the mock Western town constructed at Tabernas.

especially in the south and east of the country. The four major rivers in Spain are the Tajo, the Duero, the Guadalquivir, and the Ebro. The Tajo is the longest river in Iberia, but Ebro is the longest one to flow solely through Spanish territory and the only one to flow into the Mediterranean Sea. The three other major rivers flow into the Atlantic. The Guadalquivir River collects water from the Sierra Nevada and flows south through Córdoba and Sevilla before meeting the Atlantic at Cádiz. The Tajo flows near Madrid and then goes west into Portugal. The Duero also flows into Portugal after it passes Valladolid.

▼ The Tajo River flows around the hilltop city of Toledo. The river has helped to make the city a stronghold against invaders over the last 2,000 years.

In a World of Its Own

CREEPING ALONG CLOSE TO THE GROUND, a spotted cat is hard to see among the sand and shrubs. This is the Iberian lynx, one of the most endangered animals in Europe. Spain, unlike much of mainland Europe, still has large areas of wilderness that allow wildlife to flourish. Despite this, Iberian lynxes are found in only one location in Spain, the Doñana National Park.

Spain has a wider variety of animals and plants than its neighbors in mainland Europe. This is because millions of years ago, the country was joined by land to Africa. Over time, land masses shifted and Spain became divided from Africa by a few miles of ocean. Today, many African species can still be found in Spain.

◀ **A male lynx prowls through Doñana National Park.**

SPANISH ECOSYSTEMS

There are four main ecosystems in mainland Spain. The map opposite shows the vegetation zones—or what grows where—in Spain. The Canary Islands have their own unique ecosystems, which vary from island to island, as do the Balearic Islands. Mainland Spain is divided into the central plateau or Meseta, mountain ranges, lowlands, and coastal plains. The animals and plants vary in each ecosystem according to the elevation, or height above sea level. The large differences in altitude and climate enable a lot of different species to live in Spain. The hard-to-spot gray wolf can still be found roaming in the mountains of Galicia, while wild boar and red deer hide deep in the forests that border Portugal in the west.

Species at Risk

Over the last 30 years, Spain has worked hard to protect its wildlife. Its large size and relatively small population means there is room for both people and animals to live together peacefully. A prolonged conservation effort has helped increase the number of brown bears and ensure the survival of the Iberian lynx, although conservationists are still working to protect them and other endangered wildlife.

Species at risk include:

> Barbary sheep
> Broom hare
> Canary big-eared bat
> Canary shrew
> Garden dormouse
> Gray wolf
> Iberian lynx
> Osorio shrew
> Pyrenean desman
> Sperm whale
> Loggerhead turtle
> Mediterranean monk seal

▼ The Pyrenean desman is a rare relative of the mole. It lives in burrows and swims in mountain pools.

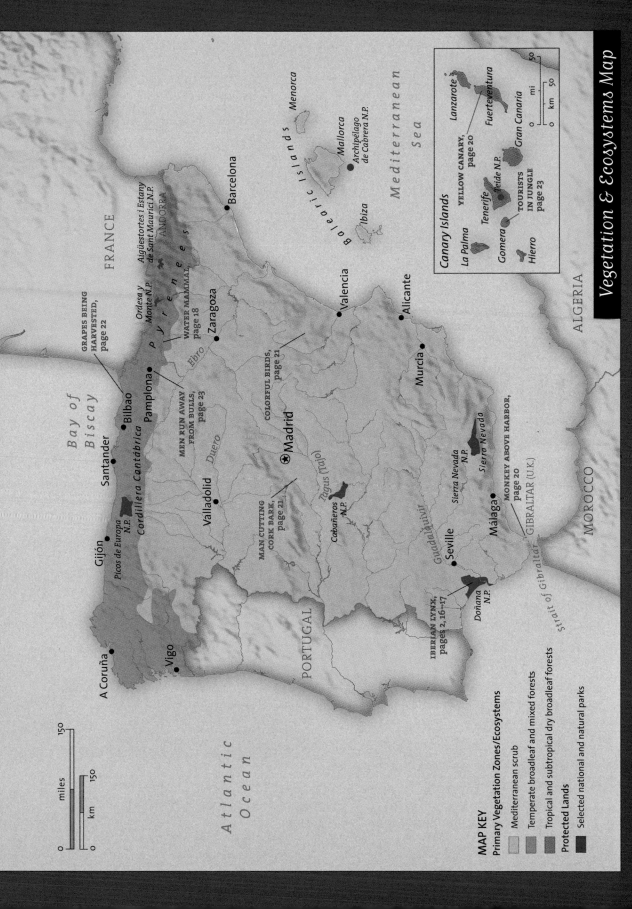

Vegetation & Ecosystems Map

MAP KEY

Primary Vegetation Zones/Ecosystems

- Mediterranean scrub
- Temperate broadleaf and mixed forests
- Tropical and subtropical dry broadleaf forests

Protected Lands

- Selected national and natural parks

miles 0 150
km 0 150

Atlantic Ocean

Bay of Biscay

FRANCE

A Coruña

Vigo

Gijón

Santander

Picos de Europa N.P.

Cordillera Cantábrica

Bilbao

Pamplona

GRAPES BEING HARVESTED, page 22

Ordesa y Monte N.P.

Aigüestortes i Estany de Sant Maurici N.P.

P y r e n e e s

ANDORRA

WATER MAMMAL, page 18

MEN RUN AWAY FROM BULLS, page 23

Zaragoza

Ebro

Barcelona

Valladolid

Duero

Madrid ✪

COLORFUL BIRDS, page 21

Tagus (Tajo)

MAN CUTTING CORK BARK, page 21

Cabañeros N.P.

Valencia

Alicante

Murcia

Sierra Nevada N.P.

Sierra Nevada

Málaga

MONKEY ABOVE HARBOR, page 20

GIBRALTAR (U.K.)

Strait of Gibraltar

Seville

Guadalquivir

Doñana N.P.

IBERIAN LYNX, pages 2, 16–17

PORTUGAL

MOROCCO

Mediterranean Sea

B a l e a r i c   I s l a n d s

Menorca

Mallorca

Archipélago de Cabrera N.P.

Ibiza

ALGERIA

Canary Islands

La Palma

Tenerife

Teide N.P.

YELLOW CANARY, page 20

Lanzarote

Fuerteventura

Gran Canaria

TOURISTS IN JUNGLE page 23

Gomera

Hierro

0 km 50
0 mi 50

 Spain's Canary Islands are named for the yellow finches that live there. These birds are the wild ancestors of the world's pet canaries.

A Refuge for Wildlife

During the last ice age much of Europe was covered in glaciers. Most of Spain was far enough south to escape the ice. As a result, species of plants that were wiped out across Europe survived in Spain. There are still 2,000 plant species that are unique to the country. They are just part of the 8,000 plant species found on the Spanish mainland and the islands. Europe as a whole is home to 9,000 plant species in total, which illustrates the diversity of Spanish wildlife.

Spanish Birds

The narrow Strait of Gibraltar that separates Spain from North Africa also makes Spain a highway for migrating birds. It is easier for birds to fly long distances over warm land than cool ocean, so millions of ducks,

GIBRALTAR'S MONKEYS

The massive Rock of Gibraltar is a tiny piece of Great Britain on the southern coast of Spain. The British inhabitants are not the only unusual residents of Gibraltar: The rock is also home to troops of barbary macaques, a type of tailless monkey (right).

The macaques are the only wild monkeys that live in Europe. They are found mainly in Morocco and Algeria across a short stretch of the Mediterranean Sea. No one really knows when the monkeys arrived in Spain. Some say Muslim invaders introduced them in the 8th century A.D.; others suggest that the Romans brought them from their African territories. The monkeys are very popular with tourists, who often give them food and pose with them for photographs.

storks, and other wading birds cross here to fly through Spain in fall.

A Dry Plateau

The flat Meseta region covering central Spain is cold in the winter and hot in the summer. Although three of Spain's largest rivers flow through the area, the Meseta is a very dry region. Most of the rain is caught by the hills and mountains to the west and north. These slopes are covered in pine trees, but down on the plain, there is not enough water in the soil for trees to grow. Instead, the Meseta is covered in shrubs and short grasses, which only turn green during the spring.

The Meseta is also too dry to grow crops; however, forests of cork trees flourish. Cork trees are types of oaks. Cork, a soft, spongy wood that has many uses, is made from the tree's spongy bark. Spain and Portugal provide most of the world's cork.

▲ A cork tree does not die when the bark is harvested. The bark re-grows in a few years.

▼ The bee eater is one of the most colorful wild birds living in Europe.

Nature   **21**

▲ Pickers harvest white grapes from the vines growing on fertile slopes near Spain's northern coast.

Forested Hills

The mountains of northern Spain are very green because they receive most of the country's rain. The heavily forested mountains are the ideal habitat for some of Spain's most timid animals, including the ibex, a type of goat. Birds of prey, such as the golden eagle, also live in the mountains. There are a total of 25 species of birds of prey found in Spain.

Fed by Rivers

Spain's most fertile regions are the lowlands around the mouths of the country's main rivers. These places are where most of Spain's crops are grown.

In the northeast, the Ebro River fertilizes the vineyards of the famous La Rioja wine, while its delta is home to many species of water birds that live in the lagoons and reed beds. In the south, the Guadalquivir River Valley is filled with vineyards, olive groves, and citrus plantations. The river's delta is a resting place for migrating birds and is covered by the Doñana National Park, where more than 300 reptile and mammal species are also protected.

Ocean and Islands

Spain's coastline runs 3,103 miles (4,964 km) along the Mediterranean Sea and Atlantic Ocean. The waters of the

RUNNING WITH THE BULLS

Every July for one week, the center of Pamplona is transformed into a crazy racing circuit. The race is like no other on Earth. Anyone brave enough can take part and run through the streets chased by six angry bulls (right). The race is dangerous; people are often injured and sometimes killed.

Bulls are an important part of Spanish life. Perhaps the most famous bull-related activity is bullfighting. Although some Spaniards think this activity is cruel, others regard the event as a glorious battle between the enormous strength of the bull and the skill and agility of the bullfighter, or matador.

Mediterranean are warmer than the Atlantic, but both support a wide array of marine life. Whales and dolphins often gather in southern waters, close to Tarifa and Gibraltar.

Mallorca, the largest island in the Balearics, is another resting place for migrating birds. Out in the Atlantic Ocean, the Canary Islands have the most diverse wildlife. For example, La Gomera is covered by a rain forest of ferns, mosses, willows, and laurels.

▼ Tourists explore the lush rain forest that grows in the misty mountains that cover the center of La Gomera.

In the Shadows of the Past

WITH THE SNOW-CAPPED MOUNTAINS OF the Sierra Nevada looming behind, the complex of the Alhambra is a spectacular reminder of the time when Spain was a part of an Islamic empire. The Moors—Muslims from North Africa—ruled southern Spain for 800 years. The Alhambra near Granada was the fortress-palace of the last Moorish rulers of Spain. In addition to leaving distinctive architecture, the Moors also gave names to many places. For example, Guadalupe comes from the Arabic for "River of Love." The Moors were the last group of invaders. The Visigoths and Celts from central Europe, the Romans from Italy, and even the Phoenicians from what is now Lebanon had already played a role in creating modern Spain.

◀ The Alhambra—meaning "the red one" in Arabic—was completed in 1353. Its many strongholds and courtyards are decorated with intricate *arabesque* patterns.

ANCIENT PEOPLES

The first humans arrived in Spain from Africa at least 40,000 years ago. Some 20,000 years later, people in Spain belonged to the Magdalenian culture. We know something about the way they lived from their cave paintings. The next wave of settlers were Iberians, probably from North Africa. They arrived about 10,000 years ago and introduced farming to Spain in 2500 B.C. In 1000 B.C., Celts arrived from central Europe and settled in northern and western Spain. The Iberians remained the main population in the south and east.

▲ These cave paintings of bison from northern Spain were made by the Magdalenian culture about 14,000 years ago.

Time Line

This chart shows some of the important dates in the history of Spain from the Roman era to the present day.

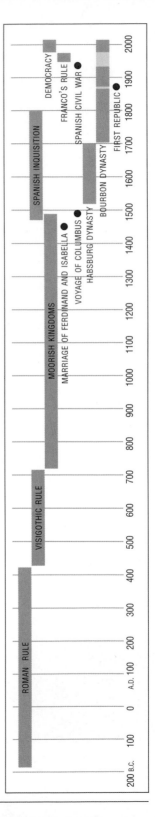

200 B.C. — 100 — A.D. 0 — 100 — 200 — 300 — 400 — 500 — 600 — 700 — 800 — 900 — 1000 — 1100 — 1200 — 1300 — 1400 — 1500 — 1600 — 1700 — 1800 — 1900 — 2000

ROMAN RULE
VISIGOTHIC RULE
MOORISH KINGDOMS
MARRIAGE OF FERDINAND AND ISABELLA ●
VOYAGE OF COLUMBUS ●
HABSBURG DYNASTY
SPANISH INQUISITION
BOURBON DYNASTY
FIRST REPUBLIC ●
SPANISH CIVIL WAR ●
FRANCO'S RULE
DEMOCRACY

FRANCE

ANDORRA

Ampurias

Barcelona

Tarragona

Pyrenees

Menorca

Mallorca

Balearic Islands

Ibiza

Mediterranean
Sea

ALGERIA

Zaragoza

SOLDIERS CELEBRATE
VICTORY,
page 34

Ebro

Valencia

BRASS MEASURING DEVICE,
page 29 AND
MILITARY OFFICER
GIVING FASCIST SALUTE,
page 35

Elx

Cartegena

CAVE PAINTING,
page 26

Alcalá de Henares

Altamira

Cordillera Cantábrica

Burgos

STATUE OF SOLDIER
ON HORSEBACK,
page 30

SPAIN

Segovia

Sierra de Guadarrama

Madrid

Toledo

Tagus (Tajo)

ARCHED HALL,
page 29

FLOODLIGHT
MOUNTAIN PALACE,
pages 3, 24–25

The Alhambra

Sierra Nevada

León

Duero

Córdoba

Granada

Málaga

GIBRALTAR (U.K.)

Sierra Morena

Guadalquivir

Mérida

Guadiana

Seville

HILLTOP TOWN WITH
CASTLE AND CHURCH,
page 28

Cádiz

GIBRALTAR

Strait of Gibraltar

PORTUGAL

Bay of Biscay

Atlantic
Ocean

A Coruña

MOROCCO

MAP KEY

◆ Selected caves with
   prehistoric paintings

◆ Phoenician colonies

◆ Greek colonies

◆ Selected Roman settlements

● Selected present-day city

Roman provinces c. 13 BC

   Baetica

   Lusitania

   Tarraconensis

Present-day boundaries, drainage, and place names are shown.

miles   150

0

km   150

0

Arriving by Sea

Spain's culture has always been linked to the sea. In the north of the country, the Celtic people spread north to Ireland, western France, and Britain. To the south, the Iberians were influenced by the Phoenicians, seafarers from the eastern Mediterranean, who set up many trading posts in Spain. The Phoenician port of Gadir was built in 1100 B.C. and is now named Cádiz.

In the 2nd century B.C., Spain became part of the Roman Empire. The region was known as Hispania (from which we get the word *hispanic*). Hispania had strong links to Italy. Even the Roman Emperor Hadrian was originally from Seville in southern Spain. Nevertheless, the Romans had trouble controlling the Celtic people in the north of Spain. In the fifth century A.D., Visigoths from France drove out the Romans. They ruled from Toledo, but were never able to control all of Spain either.

▼ Olvera near Cádiz in southern Spain has a long history. There are Roman remains nearby, and there was a large Visigoth settlement there in the fifth century. The town is still dominated by a 12th-century Arab castle, which was joined on the skyline by a Catholic cathedral built in 1822.

Invaders from Africa

In 711, the Muslim governor of Tangier in North Africa attacked the Visigoths. Within ten years almost all of Spain had come under Muslim rule. The Moors who invaded Spain were a mixture of peoples. Some were Arabs, who originally came from the Middle East, while others were Berbers, or native North Africans. The Moors called their territory in Spain "al-Andalus," from which the modern region of Andalusia gets its name.

The Moors remained in Spain for 800 years. They brought their own religion, culture, and architecture. At the heart of their territory was Córdoba. At its height, this was the most modern city in Europe, with street lights and running water. At first, the whole of Muslim Spain was ruled by a single ruler, or caliph. However, in 1031 Caliph Hisham III was overthrown, and his land was split into a number of warring kingdoms.

▲ The Mezquita in Córdoba is now a cathedral, but it was built as a mosque in the 8th century.

▼ The Moors introduced new scientific techniques to Europe, such as this astrolabe, a device for measuring the position of stars and planets.

Forcing Them Out

The Reconquest was a series of wars in which the Christian people of Spain drove out the Moors. It was started in 727 by the Christian kingdoms in the north and finally ended when the last Moors left Granada in 1492. The victorious Christian nobles kept the land they won in battle. In some cases the land is held by the same families today.

▲ Christopher Columbus visits Ferdinand and Isabella, the rulers of Spain, upon his return from America in 1493.

Uniting Spain

When Ferdinand V of Aragón married Isabella I of Castile in 1469, two of the largest kingdoms in Spain became one. Their reign is remembered for two main

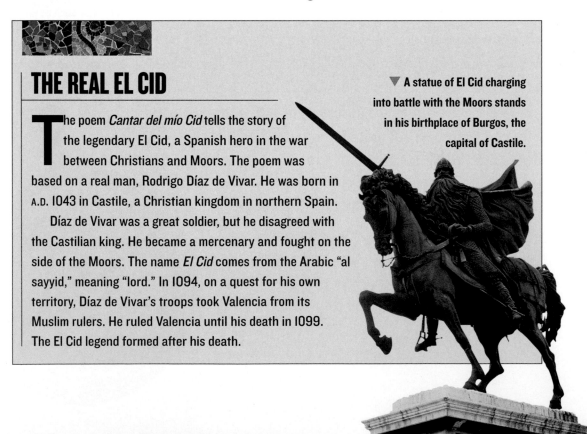

THE REAL EL CID

The poem *Cantar del mío Cid* tells the story of the legendary El Cid, a Spanish hero in the war between Christians and Moors. The poem was based on a real man, Rodrigo Díaz de Vivar. He was born in A.D. 1043 in Castile, a Christian kingdom in northern Spain.

Díaz de Vivar was a great soldier, but he disagreed with the Castilian king. He became a mercenary and fought on the side of the Moors. The name *El Cid* comes from the Arabic "al sayyid," meaning "lord." In 1094, on a quest for his own territory, Díaz de Vivar's troops took Valencia from its Muslim rulers. He ruled Valencia until his death in 1099. The El Cid legend formed after his death.

▼ A statue of El Cid charging into battle with the Moors stands in his birthplace of Burgos, the capital of Castile.

▲ During the Spanish
Inquisition people
were burned alive for
opposing the church.

TESTING FAITH

During the Middle Ages, the Christian kings were deeply suspicious of non-Christians —Jews and Moors—living in Spain. They were often forced to convert to Christianity. However, the Christian nobles still feared that they had only converted to infiltrate the high offices of power. In 1478, the Pope gave the Spanish king, Ferdinand V, the power to investigate the faith of these new Christians. The result was the Spanish Inquisition, during which people were tortured to prove that they were true Christians. Thousands of converts fled Spain as the methods of the Inquisition spread fear across Europe.

reasons. First, they paid for Christopher Columbus to explore the west in search of a new route to India and China. Instead he found America by accident. Second, Ferdinand and Isabella were devout Catholics and wanted to ensure theirs was a Catholic kingdom. During their reign, they forced the last Muslim Moors out and ordered all Jews in Spain to convert to Catholicism or leave the country.

The Golden Age of Empire

Ferdinand's grandson, Charles I, became king in 1516. He was the head of a royal family called the Habsburgs. This family had members living all over Europe, and Charles I also ruled parts of Italy, France, Switzerland, and the Netherlands. Spain had become the most powerful nation in Europe.

HEADING WEST

When the Italian explorer Christopher Columbus set sail in 1492, he had been waiting for seven years for money to finance his voyage to find a new route to India and China. He was convinced that a westward route would be faster. Five weeks after Columbus sailed from the Canary Islands, he arrived on an island he called San Salvador (now the Bahamas). He sailed to more islands and returned to Spain with some "Indians" to prove he had arrived in India. Later trips took Columbus along the coast of South America, which he probably thought was part of Asia.

After Columbus, a number of daring sailors traveled west to find new lands. Small bands of Spaniards, driven by stories of untold wealth, arrived in the Americas. Hernán Cortés overthrew the Aztec Empire of Mexico in 1522, and Francisco Pizarro brought down the Inca Empire of Peru in 1535. Both Spanish forces were very small but were able to defeat huge armies because they were equipped with guns, cannons, and horses—all of which were unknown to their opposition.

▲ An illustration from 1892 shows Hernán Cortés greeting the Aztec king Montezuma in 1519, two years before declaring war on the Native American empire.

Until the late 17th century, Spain also had a vast empire outside of Europe. This included outposts in Africa, most of the Philippines, and half of North and South America. Gold and silver from the Americas made Spain the wealthiest nation in the world.

During this "Golden Age," Spain became a center of art and culture. It was at this time that Miguel de Cervantes wrote *Don Quixote* and artists Diego Velázquez and El Greco produced their finest work.

The Fall from Greatness

Spain was the undisputed power in Europe until 1588. It then made a military blunder by attempting to invade

England. Bad planning and poor weather combined with a ferocious defense by the English led to the defeat of Spain's giant fleet of ships, the Armada.

The loss of the Armada marked the start of a new period of wars against France, England, Sweden, and the Ottoman Turks that began to gradually weaken the Spanish Empire.

The End of the Habsburgs

In 1700, King Charles II died without an heir. He had nominated Philip, the grandson of King Louis XIV of France, as his successor on the condition that the Spanish Empire was kept together. Despite opposition from the other Habsburgs in Europe, Louis XIV decided to let his grandson take the Spanish crown. This brought the Habsburg rule to an end and handed power to the French Bourbon dynasty. Spain almost immediately came under attack from Britain and

▼ The Spanish Armada was a fleet of 130 huge ships, pictured here, carrying a force to invade England in 1588. The smaller English ships were much faster, and surprisingly defeated the Armada. The fleet was forced to sail around Scotland and Ireland through a violent storm. Many ships were sunk and 15,000 Spaniards died.

Portugal. Spain lost land in Europe, and even Spanish territory, such as Gibraltar and Menorca, fell to Britain.

Lost Empire

King Philip's son Charles III restored some of Spain's greatness—and won Menorca back. Charles ruled until 1788, but his Bourbon successors were very weak and often abdicated. As Spain lost power, Britain and France grew steadily stronger. In 1805, Spain lost its control of the Atlantic Ocean when the British defeated the Spanish and French naval fleets at the Battle of Trafalgar. Then in 1824, Peru, Spain's last colony in South America, became independent.

In 1873, King Amadeo abdicated and Spain became a republic. The first republic was a disaster. It lasted a year and had four presidents. In 1874, the Bourbon kings were restored. However, Spain's decline continued, and it lost Puerto Rico, Guam, and the Philippines to the United States in 1898.

▼ Left-wing Republican troops celebrate after defeating Franco's Nationalists and Italian soldiers at the Battle of Guadelajara in 1937. Nevertheless, two years later the right-wing Nationalist army had won the war.

REHEARSAL FOR WORLD WAR

Kion vi faras por eviti tion?

GE ESPERANTISTOJ EL LA TUTA MONDO AGU ENERGIE KONTRAŬ LA INTERNACIA FAŜISMO!

In the late 1930s, Spain was ripped apart by a civil war fought by the Republicans against the Fascists. The Spanish Fascists were backed by Italy and Germany and eventually won. Adolf Hitler sent his bomber pilots to Spain to get experience and prepare for the inevitable outbreak of world war. Opposition to fascism was a worldwide cause. Volunteers from many countries fought on the Republican side.

▶ This poster is in Esperanto, an international language used at the time. The title says: "What are you doing to stop this?"

Releasing Tensions

In the early decades of the 20th century, Spain became divided as people argued about the best way to govern the country. In 1931, the king abdicated once again, and Spain was declared a republic for a second time. That did little to unite the country, and in 1936 civil war broke out across Spain between left-wing Republicans and right-wing Nationalists.

In 1939 the Nationalists under General Francisco Franco won the war. Franco became a fascist dictator. Under his rule, Spain was a poor country, and its people had few opportunities to travel abroad. Franco died in 1975, Spain became a democracy, and the Bourbons were restored as monarchs. Spain has rebuilt its economy over the last 30 years, and its people now enjoy a comfortable but also vibrant way of life.

▼ General Franco, the leader of Spain's Nationalists, was the only fascist ruler to remain in power after World War II.

Charging Forward

SPAIN MIXES THE OLD WITH THE NEW. The country was largely cut off from the rest of Europe from the 1930s until the 1970s, first by war and then by a controlling dictator. However, Spain has caught up with its neighbors quickly. Spanish children know as much about the latest fashions and crazes as any other modern child, while the way of life of their grandparents may not have changed much for decades. For example, some older Spanish widows living in rural villages always wear black, but in the big cities people rarely observe the tradition. Yet some Spanish traditions, like bullfighting, are not forgotten anywhere in Spain. Although the sport is regarded by some as cruel, many Spaniards enjoy the spectacle. The matadors, or bullfighters, are treated as celebrities.

◀ **A matador dodges a charging bull. He will try to tire the animal before killing it with a thin sword. Bullfighting is very dangerous—matadors are often injured.**

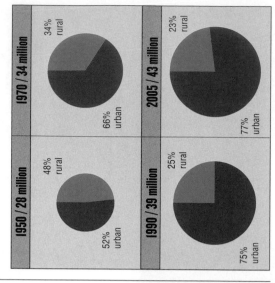

CHANGING POPULATION

Until the 20th century, Spain was a rural country. Since the end of the Franco dictatorship in 1975, Spain has rapidly modernized. As fewer people were needed to work in agriculture, many Spaniards moved to cities to look for work. The capital, Madrid, and its suburbs have the largest population with more than five million inhabitants, followed by Barcelona (more than 1.5 million), and Valencia (almost 800,000).

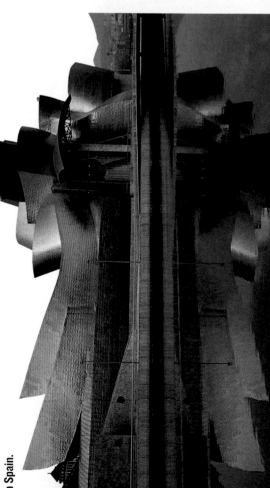

▶ **The Guggenheim Museum in Bilbao is an example of the many modern buildings that have recently been constructed in Spain.**

Common Spanish Phrases

The official language of Spain is Spanish, usually referred to as Castilian. However, six million Spaniards also speak Catalán, the language of Catalonia. In Galicia, they speak Galego, and Basques have a language called Euskera. Here are some Castilian Spanish phrases for you to try:

Good morning	Buenas días	bweh-nos DEE-ahs
Good evening	Buenas noches	bweh-nas NOCH-ez
How's it going?	¿Qué tal?	KAY tal
Please	Por favor	pohr fah-VOHR
Thank you	Gracias	GRAH-see-us

1950 / 28 million	1970 / 34 million
48% rural / 52% urban	34% rural / 66% urban
1990 / 39 million	**2005 / 43 million**
25% rural / 75% urban	23% rural / 77% urban

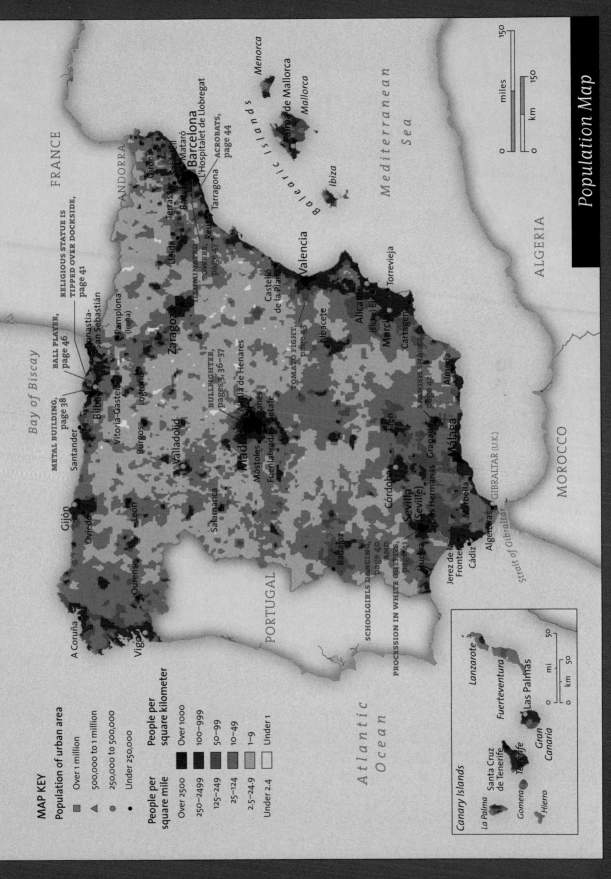

Population Map

MAP KEY

Population of urban area

- ■ Over 1 million
- ▲ 500,000 to 1 million
- ● 250,000 to 500,000
- • Under 250,000

People per square mile / **People per square kilometer**

People per square mile	People per square kilometer
Over 2500	Over 1000
250–2499	100–999
125–249	50–99
25–124	10–49
2.5–24.9	1–9
Under 2.4	Under 1

FRANCE

ANDORRA

Bay of Biscay

A Coruña
Vigo
Ourense
Gijón
Oviedo
León
Santander
Bilbao
Vitoria-Gasteiz
Logroño
Donostia-
San Sebastián
Pamplona
(Iruña)
Burgos
Valladolid
Salamanca
Zaragoza
Madrid
Móstoles
Fuenlabrada Getafe
Leganés
Alcalá de Henares

METAL BUILDING,
page 38

BALL PLAYER,
page 46

RELIGIOUS STATUE IS
TIPPED OVER DOCKSIDE,
page 41

Girona
Mataró
Sabadell
Terrassa
Badalona
Barcelona
[Hospitalet de Llobregat
Tarragona Reus
Lleida

ACROBATS,
page 44

ILLUMINATED
TOWERS,
pages 47

Valencia

Castelló
de la Plata

Torrevieja

Alicante
(Elche) Elx

Albacete

Murcia
Cartagena

Almería

TOMATO FIGHT,
page 43

BULLFIGHTER,
pages 3, 36–37

SPANISH STATUE...
page 42

Córdoba
Jaén
Granada

Sevilla
(Seville)
Dos Hermanas

Málaga
Marbella

Badajoz

Huelva

Jerez de la
Frontera
Cádiz
Algeciras
GIBRALTAR (UK)

SCHOOLGIRLS DANCING,
page 40

PROCESSION IN WHITE OUTFITS,
page 41

PORTUGAL

Atlantic
Ocean

Strait of Gibraltar

MOROCCO

ALGERIA

Mediterranean
Sea

Balearic Islands

Menorca
Mallorca
Palma de Mallorca

Ibiza

Canary Islands

La Palma
Santa Cruz
de Tenerife
Tenerife
Gomera
Hierro
Fuerteventura
Lanzarote
Gran
Canaria
Las Palmas

0 km 50
0 mi 50

0 km 150
0 miles 150

▲ Students practice Spanish folk dances in the playground at a school in Seville.

School Days

Spanish children must attend school for ten years, between the ages of six and 16. However, many children start school much younger than six. They begin preschool—*educación infantil*—after they turn three. Although school is not required after age 16, most Spanish children stay for two more years. Then, some students go to college. Unlike grade school, Spanish universities are not free, and tuition fees can be high for some families.

In most parts of the country, teachers speak in Castilian Spanish. However, in Catalonia some lessons are taught in Catalan—their students' first language.

Similarly in Galicia, lessons are often in Galego. In the Basque Country, fewer schools teach in Euskera since only a quarter of the children speak it.

Catholic Faith

Spain is a Catholic country, although officially there is no state church and all faiths are allowed. It is generally the older people who are the most likely to go to church. While the younger generation are normally baptized as Catholics, many of them do not follow the strict rules of the Catholic Church. Nevertheless, they still consider themselves Catholic and take part in the many religious festivals held throughout the year.

Most of the local Spanish festivals have a religious significance. The country's national holidays are in honor of the different Catholic saints. The importance of the Catholic faith is also seen in the many spectacular cathedrals found across the country. The most amazing is the unfinished Sagrada Familia in Barcelona.

NATIONAL HOLIDAYS

Most of the holidays in Spain are religious festivals. Great events in Spain's history, such as the voyage of Columbus, are also remembered by a public holiday.

JAN 1	New Year's Day
JAN 6	Twelfth Night (when Christmas presents are given)
MARCH/APRIL	Easter
MAY 1	Labor Day
AUGUST 15	Assumption
OCTOBER 12	Columbus Day
NOVEMBER 1	All Saints Day
DECEMBER 6	Constitution Day
DECEMBER 8	Immaculate Conception Day
DECEMBER 25	Christmas Day

▲ During Holy Week—the week before Easter—penitents march through the streets of Spain. The penitents—people who want to be forgiven their sins—hide their faces behind pointed white masks. These traditional costumes date back centuries and have nothing to do with white supremacy groups.

▼ During the festival of St. Peter on June 29, Basque fishers lean a statue of the saint over the dockside so he can bless the sea.

▲ This typical meal of tapas is served on plates decorated in the style traditional to Andalusia.

▼ Churros are a favorite breakfast food in Spain. They are often dunked in hot chocolate.

Eating Habits

In Spain, 10 p.m. is a typical time for dinner. It is also common for families to eat together, so children are used to staying up late from an early age. To fend off hunger after a long day, Spaniards eat *tapas*—snacks served in cafes and bars. The snacks are small servings of vegetables, meat, fish, or eggs prepared in any number of ways. Tapas can even make a whole meal that is eaten slowly throughout the evening.

A traditional Spanish breakfast is a pastry or a long thin doughnut called a *churro*. Lunch is often eaten in the early afternoon. After lunch people might take a siesta—an afternoon nap to avoid the hottest part of the day. However, the busy lives of modern Spaniards mean siestas are a luxury today.

Each Spanish region has its own speciality dish. For example, *paella*—a mixture of rice, seafood, and meat flavored with saffron, comes from the seaport, Valencia. Other local specialities depend on what grows in the region. In the far south, a chilled soup called *gazpacho* is eaten during the hot summers. It is made with tomatoes, bread, cucumbers, and olive oil.

THE TOMATO PARTY

If you want to take part in this festival it is best to wear old clothes and some swimming goggles! This is La Tomatina. No one is sure how it started, but today it has grown into the world's largest food fight. On the last Wednesday of August, between 10 a.m. and 1 p.m. in Bunyol, a small town near Valencia, 40,000 people throw 100 tons of ripe tomatoes at each other! The streets flow with tomato juice as everyone gets covered in tomato skins, juice, flesh, and seeds.

Fiesta!

Spaniards love any kind of festival. Even the smallest village will usually hold a fiesta, or party, once a year. They celebrate different things, perhaps a saint's day or an event in local history. Fiestas are a time for parades of floats, fireworks, and dancing. In Valencia, people create huge *ninots,* or puppets, out of *papier mâché,* and set them on fire during the Las Fallas Festival. The bull-running in Pamplona is another kind of festival.

DANCE OF THE GYPSIES

Flamenco is more than just music and dance. It is an expression of happiness, sadness, and the difficulties of life, especially when it comes to love. Flamenco is probably around 1,000 years old and started in Andalusia by the Gypsies who lived there. It blends African and Jewish dances with those of the Gypsies. The best-known type of flamenco is the *cante jondo* (deep song). The singing is accompanied by dancing with finger snapping and heel stomping. The effect of the rhythm is to create a hypnotic trance which gradually builds up to a dramatic ending.

Flamenco has influenced many of the world's most popular dances like the samba and the rumba. A female flamenco dancer (right) uses a fan and a traditional frilled dress to accentuate her movements.

Strings and Singers

Spain has a rich musical heritage. The guitar was invented in Andalusia. It was based on the lute introduced to the area by the Moors. The guitar shape we know today was invented in the 1870s. Guitars are used to play Spanish folk music.

Classical music also has had some outstanding Spanish musicians and singers, including the cellist Pablo Casals, the tenors Placido Domingo and José Carreras, and the soprano Montserrat Caballé.

Spanish pop has produced some international stars. Singer Alejandro Sanz has won 15 Latin Grammys.

▼ Acrobats form a human tower at a fiesta in Catalonia to celebrate St. Felix Day.

Julio Iglesias had hits in the 1980s, and his son Enrique followed in his footsteps in the 2000s.

▲ Spanish soccer fans show their support for the national team at the World Cup in Germany in 2006.

A Nation of Fans

Spaniards love sports, especially soccer. The two top Spanish soccer clubs—Real Madrid and Barcelona—field teams with players from all corners of the globe. The clubs attract fans from outside of Spain, too. In 2008, Spain's national soccer team won Euro 2008, a Europe-wide tournament. This was Spain's first international trophy since 1964.

In the last few years, Spain has provided some world class competitors in other sports as well. Rafael

"Rafa" Nadal is the world's number one tennis player, while Sergio García is following in the footsteps of two of the world's greatest golfers: José María Olazábal and "Seve" Ballesteros. The Spanish cyclist, Miguel Indurain won the Tour de France every year from 1991 to 1995, the first cyclist to win it five times in a row.

Great Artists

Spain's art and literature is admired around the world. During the Golden Age of the 16th and 17th centuries Lope de Vega wrote hundreds of plays and poems, mostly about love and honor. The 20th century introduced Spain's greatest playwright, Federico García Lorca. Many of his plays, including *Blood Wedding* (1933) are still performed today. Lorca is remembered in Spain not just for his talent but also because he was one of thousands executed by the fascists during the Spanish Civil War.

THE WORLD'S FASTEST RACKET GAME

Pelota vasca is a ball game that comes from the Basque region of Spain. It is adapted from a game that was played in ancient times. Today, it is also played in the United States and Latin America. The game has between two and six players and is played in a walled court, somewhat like a racquetball court. However, it can also be played on any city wall or town square. Each player has a long, curved wicker basket, or *cesta*, strapped to his hand to hurl the ball, or *pelota*, against the walls. The ball can reach speeds of 150 miles (240 km) an hour. If you get hit by the ball it can be really dangerous, so most players wear protective helmets (above).

ANTONI GAUDÍ

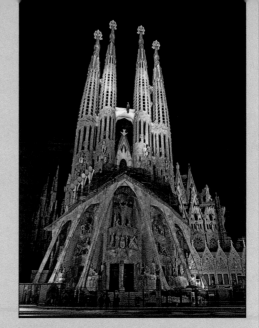

▲ The Sagrada Familia is planned to be completed in 2036.

When a Barcelona tram ran over Antoni Gaudí in 1926, nobody stopped to help the scruffy-looking man. He died from his injuries. At his funeral a few days later, thousands of people turned out to follow his coffin through the city. What they now realized was that the scruffy man was the architect of the spectacular Sagrada Familia cathedral, the most famous building in Spain.

Gaudí began work on the Sagrada Familia in 1882. The architect became a recluse and spent most of his time working on the giant cathedral alone. Construction was very slow, but Gaudí saw the project as a religious mission and refused to be rushed. "My client is not in a hurry," he once said. At the time of Gaudí's death the cathedral was unfinished and construction continues to this day.

The work of Spanish artists, such as Diego Velázquez from the 16th century, and Francisco Jose de Goya of the 19th century, continue to attract attention years after their deaths. Two of the most famous artists of the 20th century were Spanish: Salvador Dalí painted bizarre images that sometimes contain hidden illusions. Pablo Picasso had another unique style, known as cubism. One of his best known paintings is *Guernica*. It was a protest against the bombing of the Basque city of that name by the Germans in 1937.

▼ This copy of Picasso's *Guernica* hangs at the entrance to the Security Council room of the United Nations, where world leaders work to end wars around the world.

Better Times

I N 1975, SPAIN WAS A VERY DIFFERENT country than it is today. General Franco's dictatorship had produced a poor country with no democratic constitution. After his death, the country became a kingdom once again, but this time with a parliamentary democracy as well. One of the most spectacular comebacks in history was under way.

Today, Spain has transformed almost completely. It is one of the most popular tourist destinations in the world and has one of the strongest economies in the European Union. The new Spain was pushed into the world spotlight with two successful events held in 1992. The Olympic Games in Barcelona, and the Expo, a business festival held in Seville, showed the world what Spain had become.

◀ Spectators enjoy the opening ceremony of the 1992 Olympics, which not only gave a boost to Spain, but also reinvigorated the Games after years of political problems.

THE REGIONS OF SPAIN

Spain is divided into 17 autonomous communities, including the Balearics and Canary Islands. Each community has its own elected parliament and some self-governing powers. Cities have similar powers, and Spain's cities include the territories of Ceuta and Melilla, two city-enclaves in the North African country of Morocco.

For administrative purposes, Spain is then further divided into 50 provinces. The Basque and Catalan provinces have more powers of self-government than other provinces—although many of their people would like to have even more independence.

Trading Partners

Spain imports more than it exports. The chief exports are machinery, motor vehicles, and agricultural produce, such as fruits, vegetables, and olive oil. The Spaniards import fuel and chemicals. Most of their trade is within the European Union.

Country	Percent Spain exports
France	18.8%
Germany	10.8%
Portugal	8.6%
Italy	8.5%
All others combined	53.3%

Country	Percent Spain imports
Germany	15.7%
France	12.7%
Italy	8.4%
China	5.8%
All others combined	57.4%

▼ Immigrants from West Africa wait in an internment camp in the Melilla enclave. They have traveled across the Sahara Desert to reach this tiny piece of Spain on the coast of Morocco in the hope of being allowed to live and work in the European Union.

Political Map

MAP KEY

✪ National capital
◉ Autonomous community capital
● Autonomous city
• Other city

miles
0   150

km
0   150

FRANCE

ANDORRA

**Bay of
Biscay**

**Atlantic
Ocean**

Donostia–
San Sebastián
GIRL IN RED BERET,
page 54

Gijón
ASTURIAS

Santander
CANTABRIA

Bilbao
BASQUE
COUNTRY
Vitoria-
Gasteiz
Logroño
LA RIOJA

Pamplona (Iruña)
NAVARRA

Zaragoza
ARAGON

A Coruña
GALICIA
Santiago de
Compostela
Vigo

SHARKS AT
FISH MARKET,
page 56

PORTUGAL

Valladolid
CASTILE
AND LEON

Madrid
MADRID
★
KING ON TV,
page 53

Barcelona
CATALONIA

Toledo
CASTILE-
LA MANCHA

Mérida
EXTREMADURA

Córdoba
Seville
ANDALUSIA

Málaga

Valencia
VALENCIA

Alicante

Murcia
MURCIA

OLIVE OIL BARRELS,
page 56

GREENHOUSES
COVER LAND,
page 57

Cádiz

GIBRALTAR (U.K.)
Strait of Gibraltar
Ceuta
REFUGEES IN CAMP,
page 50

Melilla

MOROCCO

**Mediterranean
Sea**

ALGERIA

Menorca

BALEARIC ISLANDS

Palma de Mallorca
Mallorca
TOURISTS PLAY WITH
DOG ON THE BEACH,
page 54

Ibiza

SPORTS FANS IN STADIUM,
pages 3, 48–49

PRIME MERIDIAN

42°N
40°N
38°N

2°W   0°   2°E   4°E

CANARY ISLANDS

Lanzarote
Fuerteventura

La Palma
Tenerife
Santa Cruz
de Tenerife
Gomera
Hierro
Gran
Canaria

28°N

18°W   16°W   14°W

mi
0   50

km
0   50

Royal Democracy

Under the iron grip of General Franco, Spain endured a dictatorship that lasted from 1939 until Franco's death in 1975. Franco decided that after his death the Spanish monarchy would be restored, and the head of the Bourbon family, Juan Carlos, would be the king. The first few years of Juan Carlos's reign were filled with political upheaval. There was a failed coup in 1981 before the country stabilized, and democratic elections have been held every four years ever since.

In the 1980s, Spain enjoyed a period of rapid economic growth and was reconnected with the rest of the world. The country joined NATO in 1982 and

HOW THE GOVERNMENT WORKS

Spain is a parliamentary monarchy. The monarch is the head of state but is a symbolic figurehead who does not get directly involved in the government's decisions. Laws are passed by the elected parliament, the Cortes Generales (the General Courts). The Cortes Generales has two sections, with members elected every four years. The senior body is the Senado (Senate) which oversees the work of the Congreso de los Diputados (Congress of Deputies). The government is run by the president, who is elected by the Congreso de los Diputados after being nominated by the monarch. The president chooses vice-presidents and the Consejo de Ministros (Council of Ministers) to run the country. The highest court in Spain is the Supreme Court.

GOVERNMENT		
EXECUTIVE	LEGISLATIVE	JUDICIARY
PRESIDENT	SENADO (264 MEMBERS)	SUPREME COURT OF SPAIN
CONSEJO DE MINISTROS	CONGRESO DE LOS DIPUTADOS (350 MEMBERS)	NATIONAL COURT OF SPAIN

AN EXTRAORDINARY KING

By any measure, King Juan Carlos I has lived an extraordinary life. A few years into his reign he went on live television (right) to appeal for help in stopping right-wing army officers from taking over Spain.

Born in Italy in 1938, Juan Carlos was groomed from an early age for the Spanish crown. Franco had hoped he would replace him as dictator, but the king had other ideas. After Franco's death, Juan Carlos quickly reformed the political system and held the first democratic elections since the 1930s. His reforms angered some members of the military, which staged a coup in 1981. Juan Carlos played a significant role in defeating the coup and restoring the power of parliament. This act made him a hero in the eyes of the Spanish people, who still have strong support for the monarchy.

the European Union (EU) in 1986. The most recent election was held in March 2008, and the ruling Socialists were returned to power.

A Place in the Sun

When Spain joined the EU, it was one of the poorest nations in the union. It received money from the other member states so it could develop its economy. Spain is now the fourth largest economy in the EU and is one of the top ten in the world. As a result, it is now helping poorer EU members build a better future.

One of Spain's major sources of income is tourism. The pleasant weather combined with the long coastline makes it an attractive destination to northern Europeans who can fly there within a few hours.

▲ Dutch tourists enjoy the sunshine on a beach in Mallorca. The island welcomes more than 20 million tourists every year.

Mass tourism started in the 1950s, but it became a significant industry in the late 1970s. In 2006, 58 million tourists visited Spain and its islands. Both the Balearics and Canaries depend on tourism for the majority of their income. Foreign tourists spent $51 billion in 2006, making Spain the number two country in the world for tourism after France. Since Spain imports more goods than it exports, the income from tourism is an important source of foreign money.

A LAND APART

The people of the far north of Spain are Basques. They belong to an ancient ethnic group whose origins are unclear. Their language, Euskera, is unlike any other European language, and that contributes to the feeling among many Basques that they should be separate from the rest of Spain. The local government of the Basque country does have more power than other areas of Spain, but still some call for full independence. The ETA terrorist organization has waged a 50-year campaign of violence that continues to this day and has killed more than 800 people. ETA stands for Euskadi Ta Askatasuna, meaning Basque Homeland and Freedom.

▲ A Basque girl wears a traditional red beret and neckerchief during a festival in which Basques remember a battle with invaders in the 16th century.

Growing Inland

Traveling through Andalusia, groves of olive trees stretch as far as the eye can see. Spain is the world's largest producer of olive oil, accounting for 45 percent of the world's total olive oil production.

While agriculture is not as important as it once was, it is still a valuable part of the Spanish economy. Due to the advances in irrigation techniques, much of the dry south has been transformed into a huge vegetable garden. Among the crops grown are onions, tomatoes, peppers, cucumbers, oranges, lemons, pomegranates, apricots, limes, peaches, and apples. Bananas, coffee, dates, and sugar grow on the Canary Islands. The Balearic Islands are famous for their almonds. Spain is also the world's third largest producer of wine after Italy and France. Rioja is the most famous Spanish wine. It is produced from grapes grown in the Ebro Valley in northern Spain.

Other agriculture products include barley, wheat,

INDUSTRY AND MINING

Spain is Europe's third biggest producer of cars and other vehicles, after Germany and France. A few years ago, the country produced nearly 3 million vehicles in 12 months, although the car plants are currently producing a lot fewer.

There has been heavy industry, such as shipbuilding, textiles, and mining in Spain for more than 100 years. They were once the backbone of the economy, but today they are less significant now that tourism, financial services, and food production have taken over.

MAP KEY
- ✹ Manufacturing center
- Al Processing plant
- Steel Steel manufacturing
- Coal
- ■ Marble

Major Mines
Fe Iron ore
Pb Lead
Zn Zinc

and other grains. In 1970 farming made up 11 percent of the Spanish economy and employed a quarter of the population. Today, the industry accounts for only four percent and employs just seven percent of the labor force.

▲ An olive oil maker checks his product at a traditional olive mill that has been producing oil since 1795.

▼ Fishermen land sharks at Vigo, the largest fishing port in Europe.

Fishing Center

Spain has one of the largest fishing fleets in the world. Once the Atlantic Ocean and Mediterranean Sea were rich sources of fish, but overfishing in the last 30 years has severely threatened the stocks of fish. Today, strict EU rules are in place to protect the declining stocks. Despite the restrictions, Spanish

fishing boats travel far and wide to bring in large catches of sardines, skipjack, and yellowfin tuna.

Problems to Solve

Spain has many of the problems of other Western countries. Despite many successes against ETA, the terror group continues to launch occasional attacks across Spain, while some Islamist terrorists think the country should be returned to Muslim rule. Modern Spain has one of the lowest birth rates in Europe, and younger people might not be able to support their grandparents as they age. Spain has successfully transformed itself in recent years, and it is likely that its people will meet these new challenges, too.

SALAD DAYS

Vast greenhouses cover large areas of southern Spain. They are assembled from plastic sheeting and can be built in less than a day. They are there to provide summer vegetables, such as tomatoes, lettuce, and sweet peppers, all year round. People across Europe once had to wait for summer for a tasty salad, but thanks to the Spanish greenhouses (right), they can now eat them in winter, too. The salads are packed in bags of nitrogen-rich air. This preserves the delicate leaves as they are transported across Europe. Spain proved it was Europe's salad provider by tossing the continent's largest salad in 2007. The salad, consisting of lettuce, tomato, onion, peppers, and olives weighed an incredible 14,740 pounds (6,700 kg)!

Add a Little Extra to Your Country Report!

If you are assigned to write a report about Spain, you'll want to include basic information about the country, of course. The Fast Facts chart on page 8 will give you a good start. The rest of the book will give you the details you need to create a full and up-to-date paper or PowerPoint presentation. But what can you do to make your report more fun than anyone else's? If you use your imagination and dig a bit deeper into some of the topics introduced in this book, you're sure to come up with information that will make your report unique!

>Flag

Perhaps you could explain the history of Spain's flag and the meanings of its colors and symbols. Go to **www.crwflags.com/fotw/ flags** for more information.

>National Anthem

How about downloading Spain's national anthem and playing it for your class? At **www.nationalanthems.info** you'll find what you need, including sheet music for it. Simply pick "S" and then "Spain" from the list on the left-hand side of the screen, and you're on your way.

>Time Difference

If you want to understand the time difference between Spain and where you are, this Web site can help: **www.worldtimeserver.com**. Just pick "Spain" from the list on the left. If you called someone in Spain right now, would you wake them up from their sleep? Keep in mind that the Canary Islands are always one hour behind the Spanish mainland.

>Currency

Another Web site will
convert your money
into euros, the currency
used in Spain. You'll
want to know how
much money to bring
if you're lucky enough
to travel to Spain:
www.xe.com/ucc.

>Weather

Why not check the current weather in Spain? It's easy—go to
www.weather.com to find out if it's sunny or cloudy, warm, or cold in
Spain right now! Pick "World" from the headings at the top of the page.
Then search for "Spain." Click on any city. Be sure to click on the tabs
below the weather report for Sunrise/Sunset information, Weather Watch,
and Business Travel Outlook, too. Scroll down the page for the 36-Hour
Forecast and a satellite weather map. Compare your weather to the
weather in the Spanish city you chose. Is this a good season, weather-
wise, for a person to travel to Spain?

>Miscellaneous

Still want more information? Simply go to National Geographic's World
Atlas for Young Explorers at **http://www.nationalgeographic.com/
kids-world-atlas**. It will help you find maps, photos, music, games, and
other features that you can use to jazz up your report.

Glossary

Abdicate when a king or queen chooses to end their reign and hand it over to his or her replacement (heir). Most kings or queens will reign for their whole lives.

Architecture the practice of making buildings.

Civil war when two or more groups living in the same country fight each other for control of all or part of the territory.

Climate the average weather of a certain place at different times of the year.

Colony a region that is ruled by a nation located somewhere else in the world. Settlers from that distant country take the land from the region's original inhabitants.

Culture a collection of beliefs, traditions, and styles that belongs to people living in a certain part of the world.

Democracy a country that is ruled by a government chosen by its people through elections.

Dictator a leader who has complete control over a country and does not have to be elected or re-elected to office regularly. Dictators are often cruel and corrupt.

Economy the system by which a country creates wealth through making and trading products.

Empire territories located in several parts of the world that are controlled by a single nation.

Enclave a region of a country that is cut off from the mainland and generally surrounded by the territory of another country.

Endangered at risk of dying out.

Exported transported and sold abroad.

Fascist an extreme political system based on the racial heritage of the people living in a country. A fascist believes that only one racial, or perhaps religious, group should be given full rights within that country. People who fall into other groups are not seen as full citizens.

Geographical relating to the study of a country's landscape.

Habitat a part of the environment that is suitable for certain plants and animals.

Imported brought into the country from abroad.

Monarchy a system of government in which the head of state is the head of a royal family. The position is inherited and normally passes from father to son. Spain is a parliamentary monarchy, in which the monarch, currently King Juan Carlos, plays no role in governing the country.

Nationalist in the context of the Spanish Civil War, the Nationalists were a fascist movement who admired Hitler and similar leaders.

Peninsula a region of land that is surrounded by water on three sides and attached to a mainland by a narrow strip of land. The word comes from the Latin for "almost an island."

Republican someone who wants a country that is headed by an elected president. In the Civil War, the Republicans opposed the Nationalists, but they were made up of different political groups from Spain and around the world.

Roman Catholic a Christian who follows the branch of the religion based in Rome, Italy.

Species a type of organism; animals or plants in the same species that look similar and can only breed successfully among themselves.

Bibliography

Berendes, Mary. *Welcome to Spain*. Mankato, MN: Child's World, 2008.

Graham, Ian. *Spain*. Mankato, MN: Sea-to-Sea Publications, 2009.

http://www.casareal.es/index-iden-idweb.html (official Web site of Spanish royal family)

http://www.historyworld.net/wrldhis/PlainTextHistories.asp?HistoryID=ab50&ParagraphID=# (history of the Spanish Empire)

http://www.iberianature.com/ (general information about spanish wildlife)

Further Information

NATIONAL GEOGRAPHIC Articles

Bevilaqua, Nancy. "A Spanish Summer." NATIONAL GEOGRAPHIC TRAVELER (September 2008): 94–97

Web sites to explore

More fast facts about Spain, from the CIA (Central Intelligence Agency): https://www.cia.gov/library/publications/the-world-factbook/geos/sp.html

Known by local people as *casa dels ossos* (House of Bones), the Casa Batllo is another of Barcelona's unique buildings designed by Antoni Gaudí. Take a look inside at: http://www.casabatllo.es Click on EN for English.

The volcanic mountains of the Canary Islands are so high that they poke out above the clouds into the clear sky. That makes the Canaries some of the best places on Earth to study the heavens, and a huge observatory has been built on Roque de los Muchachos on La Palma island. It has 12 huge telescopes on it. Watch video clips about them all at: http://www.iac.es/eno.php?op1=2&op2=3&lang=en

The Alhambra in Granada is one of the most beautiful buildings in the world.
Take a virtual tour here: http://www.saudiaramcoworld.com/issue/200604/alhambra/default.htm

There is nothing more Spanish than a bullfight. Find out more about this controversial show at: http://www.andalucia.com/bullfight/home.htm

See, hear

There are many ways to get a taste of life in Spain, such as movies and music, including a Web site where you can hear a popular Spanish musician:

Enrique Iglesias
Find out more about one of the most successful Spanish pop stars at his official Web site: http://www.enriqueiglesias.com/

The Last Knight
This graphic novel by Wil Eisner is based on *Don Quixote*.

Man of La Mancha (1972)
Watch this musical adaptation of the great Spanish novel *Don Quixote*. The movie was made following the success of a Broadway stage show. Sophia Loren stars alongside Peter O'Toole as Don Quixote.

Story of Ferdinand
Read this story about bullfighting to your younger brother or sister.

Index

Boldface indicates illustrations.

Credits

Picture Credits

Front Cover – Spine: Regien Passen/Shutterstock; Top: Jean Du Poisberranger/The Image Bank/Getty Images; Lo Far Left: Jurgen Richter/Alamy; Lo Left: Norbert Rosing/NGIC; Lo Right: John Prior Images/Alamy; Lo Far Right: Kenneth Garret/NGIC.

Interior – **Corbis:** 35 up; Ballesteros/EFE: 3 left, 36–37; Bettmann: 31 up, 32 up, 33 lo; Luc Buerman/Zefa: 30 lo; Michael Busselle: 11 lo; Alan Copson; 5; Desgrieux: 42 up; Julio Donoso/Sygma: TP, 40 up; EFE: 34 lo; Owen Franken: 46 lo; Patrick Frilet/Hemis: 14 lo; Jan-Peter Kasper/epa: 45 up; Rafael Marchante/Reuters: 50 lo; Jaques Paviovsky/Sygma: 53 up; Jose Fuste Raga: 2 right, 2–3, 6–7, 24–25, 28 lo, 47 up; Reuters: 43 up; J B Russell/Sygma: 57 lo; Peter Saloutos: 44 up; Sygma; 3 right, 48—49; The Gallery Collection: 30 up, 47 lo; **Nature Picture Library:** Igor Shpilenok: 18 lo; Jose B. Ruiz: 2 right, 16–17; **NGIC:** Thomas J. Abercrombie: 41 up; James Blair: 12 up; Ira Block: 56 up; Victoria R. Boswell: 29 lo; Kenneth Garrett: 26 up, 38 lo; Bobby Haas: 12 lo; David Alan Harvey: 13 lo, 20 lo; Catherine Karnow: 15 up; Stephanie Maze: 44 lo; Albert Modvay: 35 lo; Panoramic Stock Images: 11 up, 23 lo; Joanna B. Pinneo: 22 up, 41 lo, 54 lo; James A. Sugar: 53 lo; Joe Scherschel: 21 up; Tino Soriano: 10 up 23 up; Stephen St John: 42 lo; Jozsef Szentpeteri: 21 lo; Scott S. Warren: 29 up; Norbert Wu/Minden Pictures: 20 up; **Shutterstock:** Peter Dankow: 59 up.

Text copyright © 2010 National Geographic Society
Published by the National Geographic Society.
All rights reserved. Reproduction of the whole or any part of the contents without written permission from the National Geographic Society is strictly prohibited. For information about special discounts for bulk purchases, contact National Geographic Special Sales: ngspecsales@ngs.org

For more information, please call 1-800-NGS-LINE (647-5463) or write to the following address:

NATIONAL GEOGRAPHIC SOCIETY
1145 17th Street N.W.
Washington, D.C. 20036-4688 U.S.A.

Visit us online at www.nationalgeographic.com/books

Library of Congress Cataloging-in-Publication Data available on request
ISBN: 978-1-4263-0633-4

Printed in the United States of America
09/WOR/1

Series design by Jim Hiscott.
The body text is set in Avenir; Knockout.
The display text is set in Matrix Script.

Front Cover—Top: Fireworks at the San Fermin festival, Pamplona. Low Far Left: Drummers during Holy Week, Calanda; Low Left: Nesting storks; Low Right: Lizard, Parc Güell, Barcelona; Low Far Right: Guggenheim Museum, Bilbao.

Page 1—Traditional flamenco dancers, Madrid; Icon image on spine, Contents page, and throughout: Gaudí tilework

Produced through the worldwide resources of the National Geographic Society

John M. Fahey, Jr., *President and Chief Executive Officer*; Gilbert M. Grosvenor, *Chairman of the Board*; Tim T. Kelly, *President, Global Media Group*; John Q. Griffin, *President, Publishing*; Nina D. Hoffman, *Executive Vice President, President of Book Publishing Group*; Melina Gerosa Bellows, *Executive Vice President, Children's Publishing*

National Geographic Staff for this Book

Nancy Laties Feresten, *Vice President, Editor-in-Chief of Children's Books*
Jonathan Halling, *Design Director*
Jim Hiscott, *Art Director*
Rebecca Baines, *Project Editor*
Lori Renda, *Illustrations Editor*
Grace Hill, *Associate Managing Editor*
Stacy Gold, Nadia Hughes, *Illustrations Research Editors*
R. Gary Colbert, *Production Director*
Lewis R. Bassford, *Production Manager*
Nicole Elliott, *Manufacturing Manager*
Maps, *Mapping Specialists, Ltd.*

Brown Reference Group plc. Staff for this Book

Volume Editor: Tom Jackson
Designer: Dave Allen
Picture Manager: Sophie Mortimer
Maps: Martin Darlison
Artwork: Darren Awuah
Senior Managing Editor: Tim Cooke
Children's Publisher: Anne O'Daly
Editorial Director: Lindsey Lowe

About the Author

ANITA CROY studied Modern Languages at King's College, London, before studying for a masters degree and receiving a PhD in Latin American Studies from University College. She has traveled extensively in both Iberia and Latin America. She has written numerous books for children on a wide range of subjects, including various countries of Latin America.

About the Consultants

JOSÉ MANUEL REYES, a native of Spain, is an Associate Professor of Spanish at Hanover College in the United States. His teaching and research focuses on Spain's contemporary history, literature and culture, and he has co-authored a textbook entitled *Mujeres de Hoy: Textos, Voces, e Imágenes* (Women of Today: Writings, Voices, and Images). Professor Reyes is currently writing a textbook on the "Silver Age" (1898–1936) of Spanish culture.

RAQUEL MEDINA is Senior Lecturer in Spanish and Head of Spanish at Aston University, United Kingdom, where she teaches a wide range of modules on subjects related to the Hispanic World. Her research interests are Spanish culture and literature, as well as Spanish women writers. She is the author of *Surrealismo en la poesía española de posguerra* (1997) and co-editor with Dr. Barbara Zecchi of *Sexualidad y escritura* (2002). Dr. Medina is currently working on the topic of representations of immigration in Spanish culture.

Time Line of
Spanish History

B.C.

ca 10000 Iberian settlers arrive in Spain, probably from North Africa.

ca 2500 Farming is introduced to Spain.

ca 1100 Phoenician settlers build the port of Gadir, now Cádiz.

ca 1000 Celts migrate into northern and western Spain from central Europe.

ca 200 Hispania becomes part of the Roman Empire.

A.D.

172 Moors from northern Africa begin a three-year invasion, which begins an African presence in Spain.

253 The Franks, a Germanic tribe from the Rhine, attack northern Spain.

ca 573 Visigoths invade the Iberian peninsula.

589 The Visigoths convert to Catholicism, uniting modern Spain under one religion.

711 Over seven years, the Umayyad caliphate brings most of the Iberian Peninsula under Islamic control. The new territories, governed from Córdoba, are called al-Andalus.

718 Christians from Toledo form a kingdom in Asturias, independent of Muslim rule.

777 Muslim forces defeat Charlemagne's invading armies at the Battle of Saragossa. A year later, the Basques destroy much of his army at the Battle of Roncesvalles.

1000

1000 The three major Christian kingdoms—Navarre, Aragon, and León-Castile—begin a campaign to regain control of Spain from its Muslim rulers.

1085 Alfonso VI, king of Castile, conquers Toledo, establishing a large Christian state in the center of Spain.

1179 Portugal becomes independent; King Alfonso I pushes the Muslims back into Spain.

1145 The Almohads, an Islamic dynasty from Marrakesh, take control of al-Andalus and move the capital to Seville.

1212 The armies of Aragon and Castile defeat the Almohads at the Battle of Las Navas de Tolosa.

1391 After a wave of attacks and forced conversion to Catholicism, many Jews leave Spain.

1400

1469 Isabella, heir to the throne of Castile, marries Ferdinand of Aragon, laying the foundation for the unification of Spain.

1476 After a two-year war of succession, Isabella becomes queen of Castile.

1478 Ferdinand and Isabella establish the Inquisition, a religious court dedicated to finding and punishing Jews, Muslims, and heretic Catholics.

1492 Ferdinand and Isabella complete the Reconquista; they expel all Muslims and Jews; they also fund Christopher Columbus to search for a westward route to the Indies.